THE GREAT PYRAMID

Hazel Mary Martell

RSVP

RAINTREE
STECK-VAUGHN
P U B L I S H E R S
The Steck-Vaughn Company

Austin, Texas

GREAT BUILDINGS

THE COLOSSEUM

THE EMPIRE STATE BUILDING

THE GREAT PYRAMID

THE HOUSES OF PARLIAMENT

THE PARTHENON

THE TAJ MAHAL

Published by Raintree Steck-Vaughn Publishers, an imprint of Steck-Vaughn Company

Library of Congress Cataloging-in-Publication Data
Martell, Hazel.
The Great Pyramid / Hazel Mary Martell.
    p.   cm.—(Great buildings)
    Includes bibliographical references and index.
    Summary: Discusses the building of the pyramids of Egypt, with a focus on the Great Pyramid, the tomb of the pharaoh Cheops.
    ISBN 0-8172-4918-4
    1. Great pyramid (Egypt)—Juvenile literature.
    [1. Great pyramid (Egypt). 2. Pyramids.
    3. Egypt—Antiquities.]
    I. Title. II. Series.
    DT63.M3   1998
    932—dc21   96-29680

Printed in Italy. Bound in the United States.
1 2 3 4 5 6 7 8 9 0 02 01 00 99 98

Illustrations: Mike White
Maps: Peter Bull

CONTENTS

CHEOPS'S FUNERAL

The smooth white limestone of the huge pyramid glistened in the morning sun as a procession of boats approached Giza. It was the funeral of the pharaoh Cheops. Along the banks of the Nile River, farmers and their families stood to watch the procession pass. The case containing Cheops's mummified body lay beneath a canopy on the first boat. Other boats followed, loaded with all the things that Cheops would need in his next life.

▲ The tomb of an ancient Egyptian contained many things besides the body. This model of a funeral boat was found in a tomb at Thebes.

When the procession arrived at Giza, Cheops's boat was pulled into a temple next to the landing stage. The body was welcomed by priests and then taken up to the temple at the foot of the Great Pyramid. Cheops's family and courtiers gathered to watch as the mummy case was held upright by a priest. The case made Cheops seem taller than he had been in life, but they all recognized the painted face that looked back at them. They believed that his spirit would recognize it, too.

Deep inside the pyramid, everything was provided for the pharaoh's comfort. His body would soon be in there also, and the funeral feast could begin.

CHAPTER ONE

ANCIENT EGYPT

The funeral procession for the pharaoh Cheops took place about 4,500 years ago. Cheops ruled Egypt for 23 years, from 2589 B.C. to 2566 B.C., and the Great Pyramid was built as his tomb.

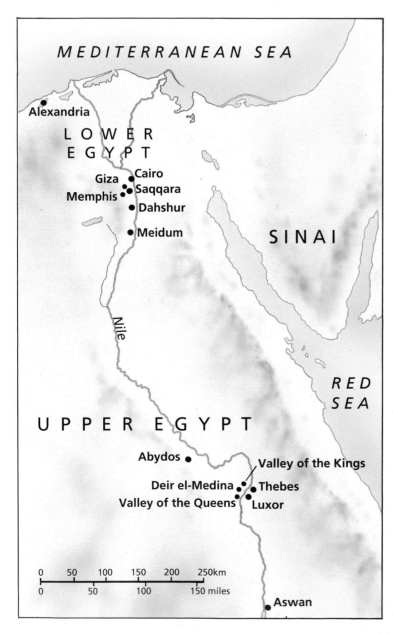

The first people to live in Egypt were nomads who survived by hunting animals and gathering wild plants. By 6000 B.C. they had begun to settle in houses built from mud bricks. The Egyptians grew wheat and barley, from which they made bread and beer. Flax was grown to make linen cloth, and papyrus reeds were used for many things: ropes, mats, baskets, sandals, and paper. Cattle, sheep, and goats were kept to provide meat and milk.

Towns and villages grew as the population of Egypt increased. Art, crafts, literature, and music began to flourish, and by 3500 B.C. a civilization had started that would last for more than 3,000 years.

◀ Ancient Egypt occupied an area on either side of the Nile River in northeastern Africa.

◄ This picture, painted on papyrus about 1069 B.C., shows an ox pulling a wooden plow. The woman walking behind the plow is sowing wheat. The same couple are shown harvesting the wheat while a crocodile sleeps on the banks of the Nile.

Upper and Lower Egypt had once been two separate countries, each with its own ruler. About 3100 B.C., it is believed that Menes, the king of Upper Egypt, conquered Lower Egypt and created one country. As ruler of all Egypt, he founded the country's first dynasty, or ruling family.

The Nile River
The Nile has always played a vital role in Egyptian life and agriculture. The landscape and way of life in ancient Egypt were probably similar to those in this modern photograph of a village by the Nile. Until dams were built recently, the river flooded every year, leaving a layer of fertile mud ideal for growing crops.

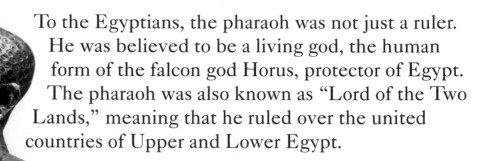

To the Egyptians, the pharaoh was not just a ruler. He was believed to be a living god, the human form of the falcon god Horus, protector of Egypt. The pharaoh was also known as "Lord of the Two Lands," meaning that he ruled over the united countries of Upper and Lower Egypt.

The pharaoh often married his own sister. Their son would become the next pharaoh and would in turn marry his sister, thereby continuing the dynasty.

The pharaoh owned everything in Egypt, even its people. He ruled from the capital city of Memphis, making sure that the country's laws were obeyed and the taxes collected. To help him do this, he had a number of ministers, the most important of whom was the vizier.

Dynasties and kingdoms

The civilization known as ancient Egypt lasted several thousand years, and nobody is completely sure about the dates of specific events. However, different periods in Egypt's history have been given names, such as the Old Kingdom (2686–2150 B.C.), the Middle Kingdom (2040–1640 B.C.), and the New Kingdom (1552–1085 B.C.). Within each period there were several dynasties—the pharaoh Cheops was part of the fourth dynasty, which ruled in the time of the Old Kingdom. Very little survives from the Old Kingdom; most of the objects and paintings that tell us about ancient Egypt come from later periods. This silver and gilt figure from the nineteenth dynasty shows a pharaoh making an offering to the gods.

The country was organized into areas called nomes, each governed by a nomarch, who was often a member of the pharaoh's family. The officials working under the nomarch were like civil servants and were very powerful people in Egyptian society. They came next in importance after priests, nobles, and high-ranking soldiers.

The senior officials had people working under them, many of whom were scribes. Scribes kept records and performed all writing tasks in ancient Egypt. They came next in importance along with middle-ranking soldiers.

Next came the craftsworkers and artists, who were in the same class as merchants. At the bottom were servants and peasants. The peasants were farmers, who could be bought and sold with the land on which they worked.

▲ Twice a year the pharaoh's officials inspected each farmer's crops and livestock, such as the geese in this wall painting. Half of everything each farmer produced had to be paid to the pharaoh as a tax and was used to feed the people who worked for him.

The Egyptians worshiped several different gods and goddesses. Every town had its own temple where the priests provided food and shelter for the spirit of the local god. Ordinary people were never allowed inside the temple, although they gathered there at religious festivals. Mostly they prayed in front of their own altars at home.

The most popular god was Osiris, ruler of the spirit kingdom. Ordinary people hoped to go to an afterlife in Osiris's kingdom when they died, but pharaohs joined the sun god, Ra.

As well as praying to their gods, Egyptians at all levels of society spent a lot of time thinking about life after death. They believed that their spirits would continue to live as long as their earthly bodies were preserved. So before burying their dead, they mummified them to keep them from rotting.

The earliest mummies
The ancient Egyptians found that bodies buried in hot sand dried out and remained whole, rather than rotting away. This body, known as "Ginger" because of his reddish hair, was mummified in this way. He was buried about 3200 B.C., with objects that the Egyptians believed would be useful in his afterlife. Six hundred years later, when Cheops was pharaoh, this natural drying process had been refined into many complicated stages.

"Hail to you, Ra, perfection of each day....
All eyes see by you;
They lack when your person sets.
You stir to rise at dawn,
and your brightness opens the eyes of
   the flock."

From a New Kingdom hymn to the sun

▲ This tomb painting shows Anubis, the jackal-headed god of mummies and embalming. Many gods were represented as part-human and part-animal. Horus, the son of Osiris, was the falcon-headed god of the sky and kings. Thoth, the god of knowledge and writing, had the head of an ibis.

The remains of mastabas, built as tombs for the pharaoh's relatives and courtiers, can still be seen at Giza. The top of the Great Pyramid is just visible behind them.

THE FIRST PYRAMIDS

The early pharaohs, their families, and courtiers were buried in tombs called mastabas. This word, meaning bench, was used because the tombs looked like the low, mud-brick benches outside many Egyptian houses. The mastabas were huge, however, with bases up to 215 ft. (65 m) long and 120 ft. (37 m) wide.

► Imhotep, builder of the Step Pyramid, was one of the first architects to design huge buildings in stone. He was also a skilled scribe, doctor, priest, and astronomer. After his death he began to be worshiped as the god of architecture and wisdom.

Most mastabas had underground chambers cut into the rock where the mummy was placed. Several chambers built over it at ground level contained all the things believed to be necessary in the afterlife. The inside walls of these chambers were often decorated with scenes from everyday life. Archaeologists have learned a great deal from these paintings about the way the ancient Egyptians lived.

The first known pyramid started out as a mastaba. The Step Pyramid at Saqqara in Egypt was built for the pharaoh Djoser, who ruled Egypt from 2668 to 2649 B.C. The original plan for a mastaba was enlarged upon several times until its base was 400 ft. (125 m) long and 360 ft. (109 m) wide. Five smaller mastabas were built on top of the base, making a pyramid that rose in six unequal steps to a height of 203 ft. (62 m).

▼ The Step Pyramid at Saqqara (built around 2660 B.C.) was probably the first large stone structure made by humans. It contains burial chambers for the pharaoh Djoser and five members of his family.

▼ The main structure of the Meidum Pyramid was built with large slabs of stone. The collapse of the outer casing, which can be seen lying on the ground around it, has revealed that it was originally built in steps. The gaps were packed with stones, and the whole structure was then covered with limestone.

The first pyramid to be built with smooth sides was at Meidum, 50 mi. (80 km) south of Cairo. It was probably completed in the reign of Sneferu, Cheops's father. The pyramid was not for Sneferu but for his father-in-law, Huni, who died in 2613 B.C. Sneferu had two more pyramids built: the Bent Pyramid and the Red Pyramid, both still standing at Dahshur.

No one knows why the Egyptians changed from building step pyramids to building smooth-sided ones, or even why they started building pyramids at all. The most popular theory is that the Egyptians saw the pyramid as a symbol of the sun's rays shining through clouds. After his death, Cheops, like all pharaohs, was thought to have climbed the sun's rays in order to join the sun god Ra in the sky.

To Cheops's people, the Great Pyramid symbolized their hope of life after death. They also believed that when Cheops joined the gods in heaven, he would work with them to ensure Egypt's safety. The Egyptians saw the Great Pyramid as a promise of eternal prosperity for their land.

"I have laid down for myself those rays of yours as a stairway under my feet on which I will ascend."

The pharaoh speaks to the sun god in the *Pyramid Texts*, religious writings from about 2340 B.C.

Other theories

Over the centuries, people have had other ideas about what the pyramids were used for. Some claimed that the pyramids were maps of stars laid out in the desert. Stars had great significance for the early ancient Egyptians. Visitors to the pyramids in early Christian times believed the story in the Bible, which said they were storehouses for the pharaohs' grain.

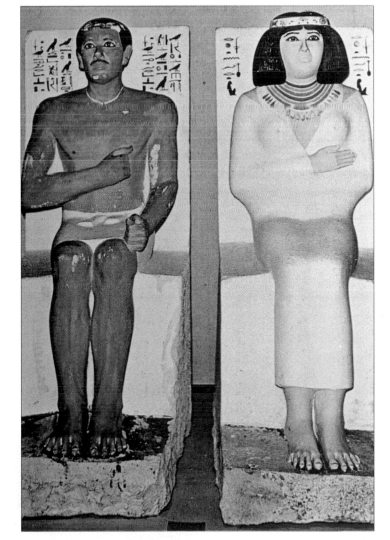

▶ Sneferu built other tombs for his family at Meidum; these funerary statues of his son and daughter-in-law, Prince Rahotep and Princess Nofret, were found in a mastaba. They are beautifully preserved, even after more than 4,500 years, and their crystal and amethyst eyes are still intact. Nofret is depicted with the pale skin of a noble-woman. Her husband obviously spent more time outside in the sun.

CHAPTER THREE

THE PLAN FOR THE PYRAMID

Cheops was the second pharaoh of the fourth dynasty, which had been founded by Sneferu in 2613 B.C. Cheops became pharaoh in 2589 B.C. after his father died.

The land Cheops inherited was both rich and peaceful. Its wealth came from agriculture and from trade with neighboring countries. Quarries at Aswan provided a rich source of fine red granite to sell. Huge cedar logs were imported from Lebanon to make into ships and sturdy doors for temples. Cheops also traded for turquoise with the people of Sinai.

▶ This small ivory figure is the only known portrait of the pharaoh Cheops. It was found without its head during excavation at Abydos in 1903, by the archaeologist Flinders Petrie. After searching the entire site for three weeks, Petrie found the head. The figure is now in the Cairo Museum.

Hieroglyphs

This is the cartouche of the pharaoh Cheops. A cartouche was used in the same way as a signature, but with the name written in hieroglyphs, or symbols. Hieroglyphs were used by the Egyptians until about A.D. 394, to write on the walls of tombs and temples and for other important writing. The oldest religious writings ever found, known as the *Pyramid Texts*, were inscribed in hieroglyphs on the walls of pyramids about 2340 B.C. To save time, everyday writing was done using simpler signs, called hieratic script.

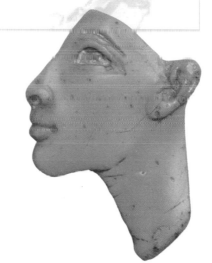

The pyramid constructed to be Cheops's tomb, known as the Great Pyramid, was built at Giza, a few miles from Egypt's capital at Memphis. It was finished about 2565 B.C. The vital statistics of the Great Pyramid are very impressive. When completed, it was 481 ft. (146.6 m) high, with the base of each side measuring 750 ft. (230 m). It was made of about 2.3 million blocks of stone. The average weight of the blocks was 2.5 tons.

▲ The Egyptians in Cheops's time used turquoise to make beautiful objects. The bottle above held eye makeup called kohl. The head is a fragment from a larger picture.

Cheops probably started making plans for the Great Pyramid as soon as he became pharaoh, as ancient Egyptians did not expect to live to old age. His first task was to choose a large, open site for the pyramid. It had to be built on the west bank of the Nile, the side associated with death and Osiris. The site could not be too far from the river, as much of the stone would be brought by boat, but it had to be above the annual flood line. Finally, there had to be solid rock near the surface to support the weight of such a huge structure.

The pharaoh chose his site in consultation with Hemon, his master builder, and with the guidance of his chief priest. Cheops would have asked his chief priest to select a lucky day for his first journey to Giza.

▶ The *Rhind Papyrus* is an ancient Egyptian document containing thousands of mathematical calculations. This fragment has to do with working out the slope and dimensions of a pyramid. Measurements such as these must have been used constantly in the construction of the Great Pyramid to achieve its precise dimensions. There is less than 8 in. (20 cm) difference in length between the sides of the base, and all the sides slope at an angle of 51.5°.

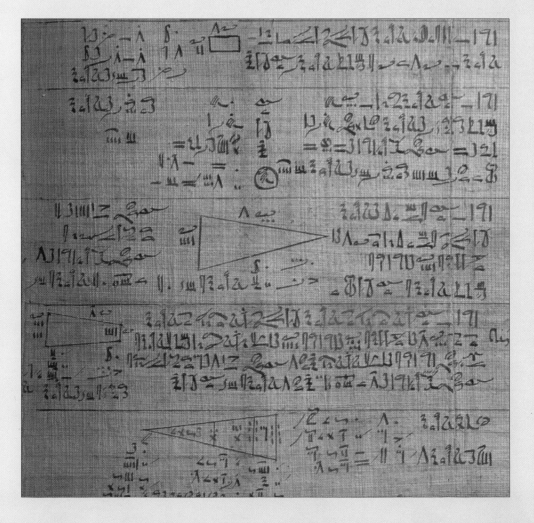

◄ This wooden carving from the Old Kingdom shows a building foreman. A foreman such as this would have been employed to supervise teams of workers on the pyramid site.

▼ This statue of Hemon was found in his mastaba near the Great Pyramid. Hemon was Cheops's cousin and probably the man who master-minded the huge enterprise of building the Great Pyramid.

For religious reasons, the pyramid was built with its sides facing north, south, east, and west. The builders had no compass and relied on the chief priest to draw a north-south line for them. The chief priest and his assistant used the Pole Star to find the true north. The assistant would hold up a special rod, or bay-stick, and the priest would move until it was directly between him and the Pole Star. He then knew that the line between him and his assistant was exactly north to south.

When all practical and religious considerations were taken care of, the four corners of the base of the pyramid were ceremoniously marked out. Hemon's next task was to assemble the men and materials that would be needed for building.

CHAPTER FOUR

BUILDING THE GREAT PYRAMID

The ancient Egyptians built the Great Pyramid without the help of wheels, animals, or machinery. Instead, a huge workforce was employed. Archaeologists think that about 4,000 skilled men worked on the construction site all year, with many others working at stone quarries, cutting and transporting stone. During the annual floods, numbers were boosted for a few months by thousands of peasants unable to work in their waterlogged fields.

Leveling the Land

The pyramid site had to be leveled before building could begin. The surveyors had a trench cut around the four sides of the site and filled it with water. The waterline was marked and then all of the rock was cut away to that level. In this way a perfectly even base was created on which to build the four sides of the pyramid. The rock at the center of the site was left unleveled and used to strengthen the core of the building.

◄ Surveyors were constantly at work on the pyramid site, making sure that the building's measurements were accurate. This stone figure from about 1500 B.C. shows a surveyor with a coiled rope, used for measuring.

The huge workforce was organized into hundreds of teams. Each team had its own name and consisted of about twenty men. They worked for six hours a day, resting in the middle of the day. The workers believed that the pharaoh was a living god and were content to work hard for him in return for just food and clothing. They lived largely on bread and beer, but were also given radishes and garlic to stop them getting ill.

The temporary laborers probably lived beside the pyramid in an enormous barracks. The permanent workforce are thought to have lived with their families in a village nearby. Many of the skilled workers would have been stonemasons, responsible for seeing that the building stones were shaped and put together properly. Others were surveyors, who ensured that the pyramid rose at the correct angle and in exactly the right direction.

"They made this for bread, beer, linen, ointment and quantities of barley and wheat."

Inscription on an Old Kingdom tomb, explaining how workers were paid

▶ The remains of a workmen's village, built to house craftspeople working on royal tombs, can still be seen at Deir el-Medina. Although this site is near the Valley of the Kings, the workers on the Great Pyramid probably had a similar village, and these remains tell us much about everyday life in ancient Egypt.

It has been estimated that 6 million tons of stone were used to build the Great Pyramid. Most of it was the yellowish gray limestone used to build the core of the structure. This came from quarries close to the pyramid. The fine, white limestone used for facing the pyramid came from quarries at Tura, on the other side of the Nile. Red granite, a very hard stone used for Cheops's sarcophagus and for the roof of his burial chamber, was brought from quarries near Aswan, almost 500 mi. (800 km) away.

▲▼ The huge blocks were cut by hand, using the simplest tools. Heavy wooden mallets (above) were used to pound chisels into stone, cutting lines and grooves. Bow drills (below) made holes by drilling into the stone with pointed copper bits.

The quarry workers cut blocks of stone directly out of the quarry walls, starting at the top and working down to the quarry floor. First, they chipped away with copper chisels to make cuts around the edge of a piece of stone. Next, they drove wedges of dry wood into the stone where they wanted it to break. The wedges were then soaked with water to make them expand, so that they split the block away from the quarry wall. The blocks were then moved onto the quarry floor with ropes and levers. There they were pounded into shape or cut to size with copper saws.

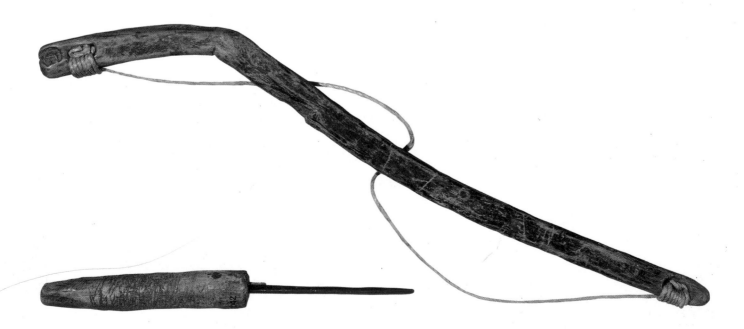

◀ Quarry workers cut and moved millions of tons of stone from the rock face without the help of hoists or any other machinery.

▼ Teams of men dragged the huge blocks of stone from the quarry to the river bank, ready to be transported to Giza by boat. The heaviest blocks used in the Great Pyramid, in the roof of the burial chamber, weighed as much as 50 tons. This papyrus painting from about 1000 B.C. shows men dragging a heavy load on a wooden sled.

At Tura the best stone was underground, and so the laborers dug tunnels to reach it. When the Nile was flooded, the limestone from Tura and the granite blocks from Aswan were brought to Giza on barges. When the first loads arrived, the building work could begin.

1. Wooden lever
2. Stone block
3. Scaffolding
4. Ramp
5. Sled

◀ Huge stones were dragged from the river to the building site and then up mud ramps built against the sides of the pyramid. The size of the project and lack of machinery means that it could have taken 20 years to complete the Great Pyramid.

The Great Pyramid is built of layers of stone blocks, each layer slightly smaller than the one below. Gaps were left in each layer wherever interior chambers and passages were planned. Apart from these areas, the whole building is solid stone.

The ancient Egyptians had no lifting machines, and so no one is quite sure how the 200 layers of stone were added as the pyramid grew higher. It seems likely that temporary ramps of packed mud were built around it in order to get the stones up to the top. The stones were dragged up the ramp on sleds pulled by teams of men. The sleds traveled over a thin layer of mud or on rollers to help them move more easily.

When the blocks reached the top of the ramps, they were dragged and lifted into position with ropes and simple wooden levers.

The great mystery
Some historians believe that one huge ramp was used to build the Great Pyramid, and that it grew in height and length as each layer was added. They believe that the spiral ramps opposite wouldn't work in practice. However, the one long ramp would have been several times longer than the pyramid itself, and there is no evidence at Giza of such a gigantic structure. There is yet another possibility—that the workers levered every stone up the sides with no ramps at all.

Inside the pyramid, a network of passages was built among the blocks of stone. The passages are walkways and airshafts leading to little rooms called burial chambers.

The interior plan must have changed twice before Cheops's final burial chamber was constructed, because two smaller chambers were built lower down in the

Inside the Great Pyramid
This diagram shows the interior of the Great Pyramid. The ascending corridor (1) leads to the Grand Gallery (2), which climbs steeply to reach the King's Chamber (3). The shaft (4) and the descending corridor (5) were used by workmen to escape to the entrance (6) when they had sealed the other passages after the pharaoh was entombed. You can also see the first, unfinished burial chamber (7), and the second chamber, known as the Queen's Chamber (8).

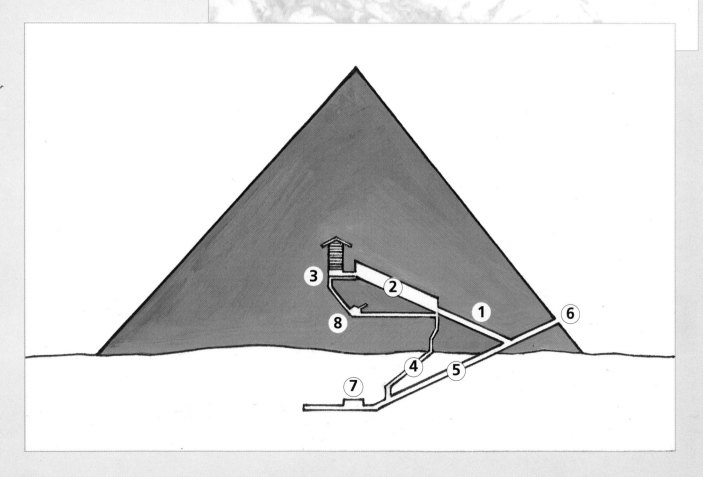

pyramid, the first one actually belowground. The third one, known as the King's Chamber, is reached by a long, high passage called the Grand Gallery.

The King's Chamber is made of red granite, with five small roofs below the top one, all helping to bear the weight of the stones above. Under these compartments lies the room containing Cheops's sarcophagus, the huge granite box that held his body. It must have been put in place while the pyramid was being built, as it is too big to have come through the Grand Gallery.

◄ Cheops's sarcophagus can still be seen by visitors to his burial chamber inside the Great Pyramid. All the treasures that were stored in the chamber have long since been stolen.

▼ The burial chamber was decorated with wall paintings and filled with furniture, food, clothes, and jewelry, made by the most skilled craftsmen and artists in the country. This wall painting from 1300 B.C. shows goldsmiths and joiners making the kinds of beautiful objects that would have been buried with Cheops, to accompany him into the afterlife.

▼ The Great Pyramid is the only one of the Seven Wonders of the Ancient World still standing today. For thousands of years it was the tallest structure in the world, until the Eiffel Tower was erected in Paris in 1887. It is still the largest stone-built structure in the world. Sadly, its white limestone casing has been removed over the centuries and used to build houses in Cairo.

When the pyramid had reached its full height, layer by layer, a ceremony took place. The pharaoh was taken to the top of the pyramid where the topmost stone, called the capstone, was laid. It is thought that the capstone may have been covered with gold, to look like the sun.

The next task was to cover the pyramid from top to bottom with an outer casing of white limestone. It was these casing blocks that gave the pyramid its smooth sides. Each casing stone was cut and shaped so carefully that it was impossible to slide the blade of a knife between two stones once they were in place. The casing was rubbed with polishing stones until it shone. As work progressed downward, the ramps were dismantled.

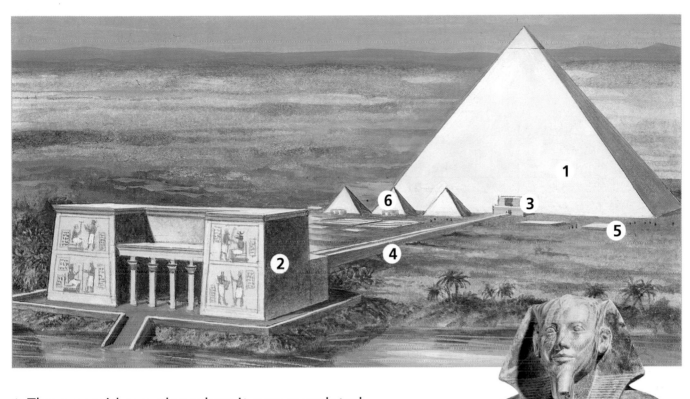

▲ The pyramid complex when it was completed
included: (1) Great Pyramid; (2) valley temple;
(3) mortuary temple; (4) causeway; (5) mastabas;
(6) Queens' pyramids.

With the pyramid complete, work could start
on the other buildings that would be needed
for Cheops's funeral ceremonies. The most
important of these were the mortuary temple
by the east face of the pyramid and the valley
temple near the river. Prayers were inscribed
on the walls of these buildings to help Cheops
on his journey to the afterlife.

▶ Nothing remains of Cheops's valley
temple, which would have contained
many treasures. However this statue
of the pharaoh Khafre was found
buried in his valley temple. Khafre's
pyramid stands next to the Great
Pyramid at Giza.

CHAPTER FIVE

DEATH OF THE PHARAOH

The pharaoh Cheops died in 2566 B.C., having ruled Egypt for 23 years. The death of a pharaoh greatly upset the people of Egypt. When he died, the country lost his protection and did not gain that of the new pharaoh until the old one had been laid to rest. Preparations for the burial could take up to three months. This was a time of deep mourning for Cheops's family, his courtiers, and all the citizens of Egypt. Professional mourners expressed the country's sorrow by singing to solemn music.

Djedefre, Cheops's son, was to become the next pharaoh. Together with the chief priests and nobles, he was

▼ This tomb painting from the eighteenth dynasty shows women in mourning. They expressed their sorrow by wailing and throwing dust over their heads.

◀ This picture was painted on the wall of a tomb about 200 years before the Great Pyramid was completed. It shows a dead person standing before Osiris, Isis, and Thoth in the afterlife. Thoth is easily identified by his ibis head. Osiris is wearing the double crown of Egypt often worn by pharaohs: the white crown of Upper Egypt is combined with the red crown of Lower Egypt.

responsible for the funeral and all of the ceremonies that preceded it. Many of these ceremonies related to Osiris, god of the dead.

The Egyptians believed that Osiris was killed by the evil god Seth, who then chopped up his body and scattered the pieces. Isis, who was both sister and wife to Osiris, searched the country for his body. Once she had found all the pieces, she fastened them back together with bandages, making the first-ever mummy.

The search from this legend was acted out as part of the ceremony when a person died. It would have been performed immediately after Cheops's death, even though everyone knew where his body was. Once it had been "found," the body was taken in a solemn procession to the Beautiful House to be mummified.

The Beautiful House was the building where the embalmers worked, preserving the bodies of the dead. When Cheops's body arrived, the embalmers set to work. First, the brain was taken out through his nose and thrown away. With a flint-bladed knife, the embalmers then cut down the left-hand side of Cheops's body. Through this cut, his liver, lungs, intestines, and stomach were removed and preserved in four containers, called canopic jars, which were buried with the body.

The spaces left inside the body were packed with a mixture of dry leaves, sawdust, and sweet-smelling herbs. Next, the body was completely covered with crystals of natron. This was a sort of salt that dried out the body and kept it from rotting.

▶ Cheops's heart was left inside his body, as he would need it when he was judged in the afterlife. This painting on papyrus shows Anubis, god of mummification, performing the Weighing of the Heart ceremony. The heart of the dead person is weighed against the truth, to see whether or not it is pure. On the left, Thoth, god of writing, is recording the judgment.

It took between 40 and 60 days for Cheops's body to become embalmed. When it was dry, the body was taken out of the natron and rubbed all over with perfumed oils and herbs, which helped further to preserve it. The arms and legs were then straightened, and the whole body was wrapped around with many layers of linen bandages. It could take more than two weeks to do this properly. Various lucky charms, called amulets, were slipped in between the layers to protect Cheops from evil in the afterlife. The outer layer of bandages was then hardened into plaster.

Once the bandaging was complete, a face mask was added. Cheops's mummy was placed in a mummy case. This was a wooden coffin, highly decorated inside and out with images of gods and goddesses. Prayers and charms were painted on it in hieroglyphs.

▶ Some mummies were placed in as many as four coffins. The outer coffin was often painted with the image of the dead person so its spirit would recognize it in the afterlife and be reunited with it. This mummy case contains the mummy of a priestess who died about 1050 B.C.

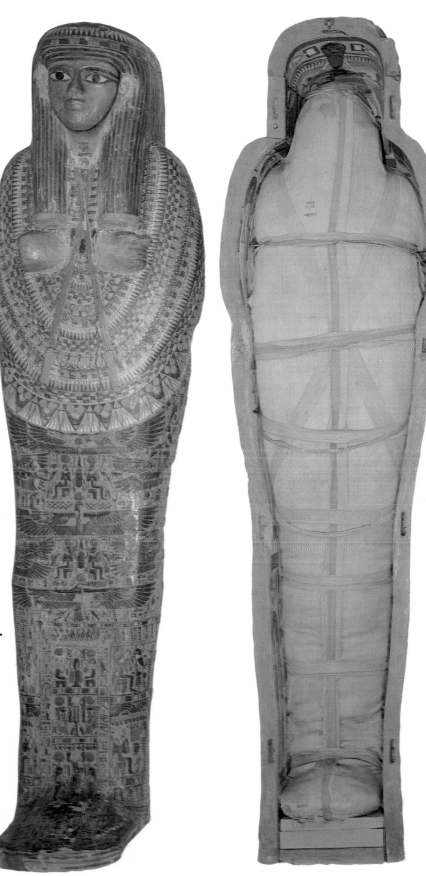

Cheops's mummy traveled by boat from the Beautiful House to the valley temple next to the river. The whole boat was dragged by oxen up the long causeway to the mortuary temple at the top.

The Opening of the Mouth ceremony, believed to bring the body back to life, was the most important part of the funeral. Once this was performed, and the priests had done everything they could to make sure that Cheops's body would be reunited with its spirit, he was taken into the pyramid.

▶ A painting from the tomb of a later pharaoh, Tutankhamen, who died in 1352 B.C. It shows the Opening of the Mouth ceremony, in which the eyes, ears, nose, and limbs were all touched with a special instrument. This was thought to allow the dead person to see, hear, breathe, and move in the afterlife. Finally, the mouth was touched so that he could eat and speak.

◄ For many years after the burial, gifts of food and drink were brought to the Great Pyramid, to sustain the dead pharaoh in the afterlife. This food offering, found at a burial site in Thebes, includes bread and fowl, still just recognizable after nearly 3,500 years.

The mummy was placed in its granite sarcophagus, which was surrounded by treasures and necessities. When the priests and mourners had left the burial chamber, workmen sealed up the tomb in the hope of preventing anyone from breaking in and stealing Cheops's treasures. They then escaped through a narrow shaft leading from the bottom of the Grand Gallery to the descending corridor, from which they could reach the entrance. Finally, the entrance was covered over with blocks of white limestone so that it was invisible.

► The Grand Gallery, now equipped with a handrail to help visitors climb up it, was completely blocked by huge stones to protect Cheops's burial chamber. The stones had been stored behind portcullises and then released by the workmen who sealed up the tomb after the pharaoh's death.

CHAPTER SIX

TREASURES OF THE PHARAOHS

"Time laughs at all things, but the pyramids laugh at time."

An old Egyptian proverb

Cheops's son, Djedefre, died just six years after Cheops and was buried in a tomb 5 mi. (8 km) north of Giza. The pharaoh Khafre, thought to be Cheops's brother, then ruled for about 25 years, and built his pyramid complex next to that of Cheops's. After Khafre died, his son Menkaure became pharaoh. He had the third large pyramid built at Giza and was buried there in 2504 B.C.

Eventually, all the building work at Giza was completed. No one stayed there except for a few priests in the temples. When they too had left, the robbers moved in. In spite of the hidden entrance and sealed passages, they managed to break in to the Great Pyramid and steal its treasures.

▼ In spite of centuries of plundering, the pyramids of Giza still rise out of the desert. The pyramid of Menkaure is in the foreground, with three queens' pyramids in front of it. Khafre's pyramid in the middle appears bigger than the Great Pyramid behind it, because it is on higher ground.

By 1000 B.C., almost every pyramid in Egypt had been plundered. Later pharaohs tried more complicated ways of making their pyramids secure. Despite using extra passages and false doors, none of them succeeded, and no more pyramids were built after the time of the Middle Kingdom. Instead, the pharaohs and their wives were buried in tombs hidden in the cliffs near Thebes. These cliffs were in two valleys, known as the Valley of the Kings and the Valley of the Queens.

▲ In front of Khafre's pyramid stands the Sphinx, a huge statue of a lion with a man's face, probably that of Khafre. Ancient Egyptians believed that lions were the guardians of sacred places. You can see that the top of Khafre's pyramid still retains some of the limestone casing that has all been removed from the Great Pyramid.

"It is sickening to see the rate at which everything is being destroyed, and the little regard paid to preservation."

Sir Flinders Petrie, arriving in Egypt in 1880

Many superstitions grew up around the pyramids and tombs of ancient Egypt. It was thought that anyone disturbing a buried mummy would be cursed and struck dead.

Many people also believed that the powdered flesh of a mummy protected a person from injury if it was worn in a container around the neck. It had long been used to treat cuts and broken bones, but in 16th-century Europe the powdered flesh was also eaten as a form of medicine. It was soon in such demand that the great necropolises of Memphis and other ancient cities were dug up and their mummies exported.

▶ It is hardly surprising that the tomb robbers were willing to risk the pharaoh's curse. This crown belonged to Princess Sit-Hathor-Yunet, and was made about 1850 B.C. The crown and the hair ornaments that were worn with it are made of solid gold and inlaid with semi-precious stones.

By the 18th century the Europeans developed a more scientific attitude to ancient Egypt. In 1798, Napoleon came to Egypt for a year. With him was a man named Vivant Denon who went on an expedition to Aswan. On the way, he made careful drawings of everything he saw. Denon's drawings provoked new interest in Egypt, but with an unfortunate result. Rich collectors and curators from European museums came to Egypt and took everything they could lay their hands on.

In 1880, the British archaeologist Flinders Petrie went to Egypt, taking with him new methods of excavation and making records. He set high standards that other archaeologists followed, and slowly people began to make sense of the huge monuments and the artifacts that were left.

▶ Sir Flinders Petrie (1853–1942) was the man who found the tiny statue of the pharaoh Cheops. He spent forty years in Egypt and excavated almost all the major sites, keeping meticulous records and making astonishing finds.

▼ Tutankhamen's body was laid inside three coffins. The outer two were made of patterned wood overlaid with gold. This is the innermost coffin. It is made of solid gold and weighs over 40 lbs. (110 kg). Inside this was the mummy, decorated with gold bands and with its face covered by a solid gold mask.

The most extraordinary find was made in 1922 by a student of Flinders Petrie, the British archaeologist Howard Carter. He discovered the unopened tomb of the pharaoh Tutankhamen in the Valley of the Kings. Carter was the first person to enter Tutankhamen's burial chamber for over 3,000 years.

The tomb had been robbed twice, shortly after the pharaoh's burial. Gold treasure, jewelry, and precious ointments had been stolen. Both times the tomb was resealed, but after the second robbery its entrance was accidentally buried by debris. This prevented anyone from finding a way back in until 1922.

◀ News of Carter's discovery spread all over the world. This picture is taken from an Italian newspaper of 1923. It shows the treasures being removed from Tutankhamen's tomb.

The splendor of what remained was still extraordinary. As well as Tutankhamen's beautifully decorated throne and other furniture, the three inner chambers of the tomb contained gilded statues of gods and goddesses, many objects of gold and ivory, and priceless jewelry.

Tutankhamen was only eighteen years old when he died, and had ruled for just a few years. His tomb was fairly insignificant compared with the pyramids, built 1,000 years earlier for the grand pharaohs of the Old Kingdom. However, the tomb's discovery gives us an idea about the even richer treasures that the Great Pyramid of Cheops may have held.

CHAPTER SEVEN

THE GREAT PYRAMID TODAY

Today the Great Pyramid stands in the suburbs of Cairo, which has replaced Memphis as the capital of Egypt. Thousands of people from all over the world visit the Giza pyramids every day.

◄ Cheops's funeral boat was buried in a boat pit next to the Great Pyramid, just after his burial. It was discovered in 1954 by an Egyptian archaeologist. More than 650 pieces of timber were found, one with Cheops's name carved on it. The timber was pieced together to recreate this elegant boat, now on display in a museum beside the pyramid.

Scientific excavation continues in and around the pyramid, and many discoveries have been made over the last 75 years. In 1925, the tomb of Queen Hetepheres, Cheops's mother, was discovered at Giza. It contained a fine collection of jewelry and furniture. In 1991, workmen digging a new sewer discovered the remains of Cheops's valley temple. The site cannot be excavated at the moment because there are houses on top of it.

In 1993, a small camera on a robot was sent along two tiny passages inside the Great Pyramid. The camera's journey revealed that a previously unexplored passage from the Queen's Chamber was blocked by a small portcullis with copper handles. What lies beyond it is still a secret, 4,500 years after the Great Pyramid was built.

▼ Exhaust fumes from tourist buses and the roads of Cairo's busy suburbs are beginning to damage the ancient stones of the pyramids.

TIME LINE

4000–2601 B.C.

3400 Towns develop along banks of Nile River

3100 Upper and Lower Egypt united. Menes builds capital at Memphis

2686 Old Kingdom period begins

2649 Djoser buried in Step Pyramid at Saqqara

2613 Huni buried in pyramid at Meidum

2600–2001 B.C.

2589 Sneferu dies and Cheops becomes pharaoh

2566 Cheops buried in Great Pyramid. Djedefre becomes pharaoh

2561 Khafre becomes pharaoh

2532 Khafre buried in his pyramid at Giza. Menkaure becomes pharaoh

2504 Menkaure buried in his pyramid at Giza

2181 Old Kingdom collapses after flooding and famine

2040 Middle Kingdom period begins. New capital at Thebes

2000–1001 B.C.

1782 Middle Kingdom collapses

1570 New Kingdom period begins

1070 New Kingdom collapses. Egypt invaded by Assyrians, Nubians, and Persians

1000–1 B.C.

525 Egypt becomes part of Persian empire

332 Alexander the Great conquers Egypt and founds Alexandria

305 Ptolemies come to power

30 Romans defeat Cleopatra, last of the Ptolemies. Egypt becomes part of Roman empire

A.D. 1–1800

641 Egypt becomes part of Islamic world. Stone removed from pyramids to construct mosques

1500–1600 Powdered mummies exported to Europe

1798 Napoleon sends Denon's expedition to record Egyptian monuments

A.D. 1800–2000

1880 Archaeologist Flinders Petrie makes scientific study of Great Pyramid

1922 Discovery of Tutankhamen's tomb

1925 Tomb of Hetepheres excavated

1954 Discovery of Cheops's funeral boat

1991 Remains of Cheops's valley temple discovered

1993 Camera sent to explore small passages inside Great Pyramid

INDEX